Raspberry Pi Manual for Beginners

Step-by-Step Guide to the first Raspberry Pi Project including 25 Video Lessons

Axel Mammitzsch

Copyright © 2019 Axel Mammitzsch

All rights reserved.

Imprint: Independently published

Impressum:

Axel Mammitzsch
c/o AutorenServices.de
Birkenallee 24
36037 Fulda / Germany
raspi-config.com

Table of Contents

1. Introduction 8
2. What is a Raspberry Pi? 9
   Goal of the Development 10
3. Which Projects exist already? 11
   Project: LibreELEC Media Center 11
   Project: Homebridge 12
   Project: MagicMirror 13
   Project: Pi-Hole Ad-Blocker 14
   Project: RetroPi Game-Console 14
4. Which Raspberry Pi models are available and which is right for me? 15
   Raspberry Pi 4 15
   Raspberry Pi 3B+ 15
   Raspberry Pi 3A+ 16
   Raspberry Pi Zero 17
   Raspberry Pi Compute Module 17
5. Raspberry Pi + Accessoires 19
   Raspberry Pi 3B+ / 4 19

Micro-SD Card *19*

Camera-Module *20*

Sensors and Modules *20*

Official Raspberry Pi power supply *21*

Raspberry Pi 3B+ Starter Kit *21*

6. Technical Data and Interfaces 22

Serial Interface *22*

System-on-a-Chip (SoC) *22*

Processor (CPU) *23*

Main Memory (RAM) *23*

Composite Audio & Videointerface *23*

Micro-USB Connection *23*

40 PIN Connector *24*

USB Ports & Network *24*

Micro-SD Connection *24*

7. What can I do after the first start? 25

User Interface *25*

Internet Browser *25*

File Management *25*

Standard-Software *26*

	Programming	*26*
	Python	*27*
8.	**Download the Operating System**	**28**
	NOOBS	*28*
	Image with Desktop and recommended Software	*29*
	Image with Desktop without Software	*29*
	Image without Desktop and Software	*29*
	Image for installation on your PC	*30*
	More Operating System Images	*30*
9.	**Installation of the OS with Etcher (PC+Mac)**	**31**
10.	**Installation with NOOBS**	**32**
11.	**Setup with a Monitor**	**35**
	First Boot	*35*
	Set the User und Password	*35*
	WLAN-Configuration	*36*
12.	**Setup without a Monitor**	**36**
	Download the Image	*37*
	Activate SSH	*37*
	Find the IP-Address	*38*

Access over the Terminal *39*

Country Settings *40*

VNC Remote Access *40*

Remote Control with RealVNC Viewer *41*

Complete the Setup *41*

13. Backup & Restore (SD-Card) **42**

For Mac – Apple Pi Baker *42*

For PC – Win 32 Disk Imager *43*

14. MicroSD Card deletion **44**

15. Software Projects **46**

Pi-Hole *46*

Homebridge *46*

Webmin *46*

16. Projekt: Pi-Hole **48**

17. Project: Homebridge **52**

18. Project: Webmin **55**

19. Project: RetroPi + KODI **57**

20. Hardware Projects **61**

21.	Project: Camera-Module	63
22.	Project: Humidity Sensor	66
23.	Project: Light Sensor	70
24.	Project: Laser Module	72
25.	Video: Programming with Scratch	75
26.	Video: Programming with Thonny	75
27.	**100 Quiz-Questions**	**75**
	Quiz-Answers	*99*
28.	Access to the Video Lessons	**108**

1. Introduction

Thank you very much for choosing the Raspberry Pi beginners guide including 25 exciting video lessons!

In this tutorial, I will explain how to install and configure the Raspberry Pi 3B+ and much more. Since its release I have been enthusiastic about the Raspberry Pi and everything what you can do with it.

In this book, I would like to make my collected knowledge and experiences available to all Raspberry Pi beginners. This Raspberry Pi manual is conceived as a compact introduction for all beginners who would like to have a simple and understandable manual to quickly get into the subject.

I will explain step by step how to do the installation process, and how to work with the Raspberry Pi and its applications for the first time. There will be even a few small software and hardware projects covered later.

Since I want to introduce you to the Raspberry Pi as soon as possible, we will first discuss the history and background of the Raspberry Pi. Then we'll go through all currently available models, technical data, interfaces, interesting projects, and available operating systems.

This is followed by easily implementable software projects and small programming tasks. At the end, I'll tell you some of my favorite projects to copy. After completing these instructions, you would have learned so much about the Raspberry Pi that you can set up a Raspberry Pi independently and become creative with your own projects.

This tutorial is for Raspberry Pi beginners who want to build up or expand their knowledge. If your goal is to use a Raspberry Pi to create projects for your everyday or professional use, then this manual is perfect for you.

Thank you for choosing this Raspberry Pi manual. I hope I made you curious already. If you'd like to learn more about the Raspberry Pi, read another chapter or take a look at the first video lesson at www.raspi-config.com right now. You can find the access data on the last page of this book.

Would you like to watch this book chapter as a video? Then log into the access area at www.raspi-config.com/amazon now. You can find the access data on the last page as mentioned.

2. What is a Raspberry Pi?

I would like to briefly introduce the Raspberry Pi and its backgrounds to you. In order to further work with the Raspberry Pi, it is important that you understand the intention and idea behind this computer.

The Raspberry Pi was developed by the Raspberry Pi Foundation in England and the first device was launched in early 2012. To this date, many versions of the Raspberry Pi have been released and have continuously improved with each version.

There are even industrial models and versions that have become smaller and smaller, such as the Raspberry Pi Zero. By the end of 2017, more than 17 million Raspberry Pi units had already been sold.

Goal of the Development

The goal of the Raspberry Pi Foundation is to introduce young people to hardware and software programming and to facilitate their entry into programming.

The Raspberry Pi is relatively inexpensive to buy and therefore the entry barriers to development with the Raspberry Pi are very low. The special thing about the Raspberry Pi is that this small credit card format hides a full-fledged computer.

In the meantime, numerous projects for everyday and professional life can be implemented very easily. The Raspberry Pi Foundation also plays an important role here. On the website raspberrypi.org you can find numerous suggestions for very ambitious projects, which can be easily rebuilt.

The Raspberry Pi Foundation also carries out numerous school projects to introduce young students into programming. Since there are many different kinds of software and hardware based on Raspberry Pi projects out there, I would like to showcase some of them in the next chapter.

So much can be said in advance, as there are now entire business models and commercial devices based on a Raspberry Pi. This already shows that the Raspberry Pi has become very widespread and is no longer just a learning device for young people.

Would you like to watch this book chapter as a video? Then log into the access area at www.raspi-config.com/amazon now. You can find the access data on the last page.

3. Which Projects exist already?

In this chapter, I would like to introduce you to Raspberry Pi projects which have already been implemented with the Raspberry Pi software and are also very easy to recreate. These are exclusively software-based projects.

Project: LibreELEC Media Center

The first project I want to introduce is LibreELEC (libreelec.tv). LibreELEC is a multimedia center which you can turn just about any TV into a smart TV. You can use it to download apps, access hard disks, and play movie files from the remote PC on the TV.

You can also receive internet radio broadcasts and stream them to your sound system. Additionally, there is a Spotify app for LibreELEC, if you have an account. This is a project where Raspberry Pi can make itself useful in everyday life.

Project: Homebridge

An interesting project in the area of Smart-Home is the project Homebridge (homebridge.io). This software-based project is relatively easy to implement. By using Homebridge, even non-Apple certified Smart-Home devices can be used with Apple's HomeKit and be controlled without any additional apps.

The whole thing can be implemented very easily with a Raspberry Pi. The practical thing about it, is that the software is relatively easy to install and control. This means that you only have to add plug-ins from different manufacturers and then control them directly via Apple's HomeKit.

The picture below shows two virtual lamps that can be switched on and off directly. You can easily add such devices later in HomeKit with a simple QR code. Just scan the code with the photo app and you can control the device from your iPhone, iPad or even your Mac.

And the whole thing is very easy to install. This will be discussed later in this manual.

Project: MagicMirror

Another interesting project from the area of Smart-Home is the project MagicMirror (magicmirror.builders). The software is relatively easy to install. You can use it to set up a display in the mirror, which you can hang in your house or apartment. In the mirror you can display various information, such as time and weather. The mirror can also be connected to other Smart-Home devices. So the project is a very nice gimmick, which can be easily realized with a little tinkering.

Project: Pi-Hole Ad-Blocker

Another useful project we will look at in this book is the Pi-Hole project (pi-hole.net). Pi-Hole is a network-wide advertising blocker that can be installed on the Raspberry Pi.

If you redirect the Internet settings on your router to Pi-Hole, all Internet traffic will be filtered through the Raspberry Pi. From this point on, the pi-hole server will ensure that, for example, most advertisements on each device are filtered out. We will take a closer look at this later in the book to see how it works in detail.

Project: RetroPi Game-Console

As the last project I would like to introduce RetroPi (retropie.org.uk) to you. This is a special operating system where old arcade and console games up to Playstation 1 can be emulated and played on the Raspberry Pi. This project is a nice opportunity to recreate on your free time or to spend time with your kids.

Would you like to watch this book chapter as a video? Then log into the access area at www.raspi-config.com/amazon now. You can find the access data on the last page.

4. Which Raspberry Pi models are available and which is right for me?

In this chapter, I would like to explain the different models of the Raspberry Pi, in order to give you a recommendation of which model is perhaps the best for you.

Raspberry Pi 4

This is the current model of the Raspberry Pi introduced in July 2019. It comes with two micro HDMI ports instead of one normal sized HDMI port like in the past models. The main differences between the past models are the processors and the RAM.

Since this course is built around the Raspberry Pi 3B+, I will explain that model in more detail. The Raspberry Pi 4 is available in a 1GB, 2GB, and 4GB model. The processor is also new and clocks at 1,5Ghz instead of 1,4Ghz in the 3B+ model.

Raspberry Pi 3B+

The model 3B+ is the second to last model and has the following connections on the mainboard.

- DSI Camera Port
- Broadcom BCM2837BO SoC - System on a Chip
- CPU: 64bit, 4 cores, 1,4GHz (up to 70 Degrees)

- up to 80 degrees 1,2GHz
- over 80 degrees clocking automatically downwards
- RAM: 1GB
- GPU: 400MHz Video Core IV
- 1080p HDMI
- 3.5mm audio connector
- A/V & 5V Power
- Standard Pi 40 Pin GPIO
- 4 Pin improved PXE Ethernet booting / Power over Ethernet (PoE)
- Wifi Chip 802.11ac + Bluetooth 4.2
- 4x USB 2.0 ports + Gigabit network port
- Gigabit Ethernet internally connected via USB, so "only" 300MBit/s
- microSD Cards Slot
- Power consumption: 3W under full load
- Tip: Audio connection is at the same time composite video connection

Raspberry Pi 3A+

The second model currently available is the Raspberry Pi 3A+. The 3A+ was launched in December 2018 and this model is the further development of the 3A model. The 3A+ has similar values as the latest Raspberry Pi 3B+.

It is also 1.4 gigahertz fast and has a total of four CPU cores on the processor. However, the 3A+ has significantly fewer connections. For example, there is only one USB port on the board. There is also an HDMI output and a micro-

USB port for the power supply. They are the same interfaces as with the 3B+ for the displays and cameras. The PINs for connecting additional sensors are also available on the 3A+. The two models 3B+ and 3A+ are currently the two standard models on the market, which are both in similar price ranges.

Raspberry Pi Zero

The Raspberry Pi Zero is special in its own manner, because of its incredibly compact size that it takes up much less space. It is incredibly useful when constructing projects that have a physical limit.

The Raspberry Pi Zero has only 1 gigahertz on one core in the processor. There are also significantly fewer connections and there is only one mini HDMI port, for which you first need a suitable HDMI adapter.

In addition, there are two micro-USB ports that can be used to connect more devices. Unfortunately, there are no other interfaces on the Raspberry Pi Zero. However, there is also the possibility to connect PINs via adapters. This means that you really have the simplest Raspberry Pi variant, but it already offers some possibilities for projects.

Raspberry Pi Compute Module

In the meantime, the Raspberry Pi Foundation has also launched an industrial model. The so-called Raspberry Pi Compute Module. These models are intended for the installation in different devices and therefore have clearly different technical values. The compute modules have only 1.2 gigahertz, slightly less than the 1.4 Ghz of the Raspberry Pi 3B+ and 3A+ model.

The Compute Module still has a quad-core processor integrated. The special feature of this model is that the memory is not on an SD card, but built in directly. This means that you don't need to buy an additional memory unit.

We have the Raspberry Pi models 3B+, 3A+, which differ only slightly in the USB connections and the processor clock. We have the Raspberry Pi Zero (without WLAN) and Zero W (with WLAN & Bluetooth). And we have the Compute Module for industrial use.

Which model is best for you now? The model 3B+ is the best suited for beginners and is currently the standard model. With it you have all possibilities to start immediately. With the model 3A+ has approximately the same performance standard; you simply have the problem of missing USB ports which can lead to problems sooner or later. Especially if you want to connect a mouse and keyboard.

This means that the 3A+ model is more likely to be used remotely and without a monitor. So for this manual, the 3B+ is probably the best model for you.

Would you like to watch this book chapter as a video? Then log into the access area at www.raspi-config.com/amazon now. You can find the access data on the last page.

5. Raspberry Pi + Accessoires

After we discussed which versions and models of the Raspberry Pi are available. I would like to briefly explain where you can buy a Raspberry Pi, its accessories, and which accessories are recommended.

Raspberry Pi 3B+ / 4

The Raspberry Pi 3B+ is already mentioned as the best model for this course and is available at Amazon. But it can also be purchased at many other sites. Link to the Raspberry Pi 3B+ (Affiliate Link) - https://amzn.to/30krhSd or Raspberry Pi 4 https://amzn.to/2R5dwnG if you like to choose that model.

Micro-SD Card

In addition to the Raspberry Pi you need a Micro SD card. I recommend a 32 Gigabyte SD card, becasue it is big enough for your storage capacity needs. This is also available at Amazon. Link to the 32GB SD card (Affiliate Link) - https://amzn.to/2WJkGOR

An important note is, when you buy an SD card, pay attention to the classification. The card mentioned above has the class 10, which is necessary to ensure a reliable reading and writing speed. So be sure to check it if you buy another card other than my recommendation.

Camera-Module

The Raspberry Pi can be expanded with the camera module, which was officially developed by the Raspberry Pi Foundation. You can find this module either on the official Raspberry Pi website (raspberrypi.org) or also on Amazon. Link to the official Raspberry Pi camera module (Affiliate Link) - https://amzn.to/30kvSnr

By the way, there are two different versions of the camera module. There is one version with infrared sensor and one without. The main difference between the two is that you can use the camera at night as an infrared surveillance camera.

Sensors and Modules

Another very useful extension is the sensor package from SunFounder. It contains 37 sensors for different applications and contains numerous extensions for the Raspberry Pi and its applications, like for example a remote control, or a small LCD display. It is important to note, there are also sensors of all kinds, including a plug-in board and cable connections. You can use it to carry out a whole host of experiments and projects. Link to the 37 Sensors Starter Kit from SunFounder (Affiliate Link) - https://amzn.to/2LHpnrx

Another recommended package is the 39 Sensors Starter Kit from Quimat. They have different types of sensors, small displays, temperature sensors, light sensitivity sensors and so on and so forth are included. Link to the 39 Sensor Kit from Quimat (Affiliate Link) - https://amzn.to/2WNDHQk

Official Raspberry Pi power supply

A very important topic you should not neglect is the power supply for the Raspberry Pi. Theoretically, you can connect any Micro-USB charger cable to the Raspberry Pi. However, the Raspberry Pi only tolerates a certain voltage, or must have a certain voltage, in order to function at all.

Otherwise, you will get a permanent "Undervoltage Error Message" on your screen. This indicates that the power supply is too low and it cannot run with a limited CPU clock.

For example, I use my Raspberry Pi with an iPad charger, because it has enough voltage. The Raspberry Pi Foundation has an official power supply that you can order here. Link to the official Raspberry Pi power supply (Affiliate Link) - https://amzn.to/2LKaEw9

However, there are now chargers from numerous other manufacturers that you can use to operate the Raspberry Pi. Of course it is always advisable to use the official power supply as it is recommended for safety and so on.

Raspberry Pi 3B+ Starter Kit

So far, the overview of this section is about Raspberry Pi accessories and where you can buy a Raspberry Pi as a starter kit. In general, of course, there are many Raspberry Pi starter packs, where you can find all sorts of accessories.

It is also worth comparing the prices for single purchases. Included are a charger, a micro-SD card and additional cases for the Raspberry Pi, if you don't want to have the board open? Link to the Raspberry Pi 3B+ Starter Kit (Affiliate Link) - https://amzn.to/30nXlVs

Would you like to watch this book chapter as a video? Then log in to the access area at www.raspi-config.com/amazon now. You can find the access data on the last page.

6. Technical Data and Interfaces

In this chapter, I will explain the components and technical data of the Raspberry Pi. I will also explain the entire technical aspects with the Raspberry Pi 3B+.

Serial Interface

There are two so-called serial interfaces on the board. The first one is for an LCD display and the second one is for the official Raspberry Pi camera.

System-on-a-Chip (SoC)

There is a chip from Broadcom on the circuit board, called a System-on-a-Chip. A System-on-a-Chip is a chip with all necessary modules for a computer like the main processor, main memory, sound, and graphics processor. All these modules are combined on one chip.

Processor (CPU)

The processor has a 64-bit with four cores and operates at 1.4 gigahertz per core up to 70 degrees. Depending on the operating temperature, the clock is automatically set further down. Once the temperature is up to 80 degrees, it is then only 1.2 GHz per processor core. Over 80 degrees, the clock then automatically goes down further and further.

Main Memory (RAM)

The main memory (RAM), which is also located on the SoC, is 1 gigabyte and the graphics processor operates at 400 megahertz per second. Furthermore, an HDMI output is built in, which can reproduce a resolution of 1080p in FullHD.

Composite Audio & Videointerface

The Raspberry Pi 3B+ also has a 3.5 mm audio connector, which is also a composite video connector. If you are not able to use the HDMI output, this is an alternative way to output the video signal via this video output.

Micro-USB Connection

In front of the Raspberry Pi 3B+ is the Micro-USB connector for the power supply with alternating current and 5 Volt. It is recommended to connect the official Raspberry Pi power supply as previously mentioned.

40 PIN Connector

The sensors and modules can still be connected to the 40 PIN input and output contacts in order to work with them on the hardware side. On the chip with the raspberry is the WiFi chip with the standard 802.11ac. The Bluetooth version 4.2 is also integrated on the same chip.

USB Ports & Network

The Raspberry Pi 3B+ has four USB 2.0 ports and a 1 Gigabit network port next door. However, the network port is internally connected via USB and thus has a real speed of only 300 MBit per second. As far as the network connection is concerned, it must also be mentioned that this is a Power-over-Ethernet-capable connection. This means that the power can be supplied via this port and the Raspberry Pi can be started remotely via this port.

Micro-SD Connection

Otherwise, a micro SD card slot is installed under the motherboard, which serves as hard disk storage. The Raspberry Pi 3B+ has a power consumption of approx. 3-5 watts under full load. That is habout 7-8 Euro per year if it would run through every day. The operating costs are therefore very limited. So much for the technical data of the Raspberry Pi 3B+.

Would you like to watch this book chapter as a video? Then log into the access area at www.raspi-config.com/amazon now. You can find the access data on the last page.

7. What can I do after the first start?

In this chapter, I would like to explain what you can do with the Raspberry Pi after the first operating system start.

User Interface

First, a very important fact, which I would like to clarify in advance. The Raspberry Pi has its own operating system (Raspbian), which is based on Debian Linux and has a normal graphical user interface, like how you are used to from other operating systems. That's why you can do a lot with a Raspberry Pi right from the start.

Internet Browser

There is also a normal Internet browser, with which you can surf the Internet immediately once the WLAN connection has been established. By the way, the Internet browser is based on a version of Google Chrome.

File Management

There is also a file explorer where you can browse the files stored on the SD card, just like any other computer.

Standard-Software

There is the pre-installed standard software such as the calculator, terminal, a program to open PDF files, the task manager, text editors, and so on. Also on board is a complete Office package from LibreOffice, with which you can open normal Office files such as .doc and .xls files.

All this works in a pleasant speed on the Raspberry Pi, even though the computer is so incredibly small. Furthermore there are other programs on the Raspberry Pi like the VLC Media Player which you can use directly.

Programming

Another pre-installed program is Scratch. With Scratch we better understand the idea behind the Raspberry Pi Foundation, i.e. the simple approach of topics like programming. With Scratch you can easily develop programs with text modules that you can simply drag and drop.

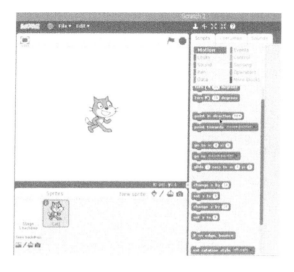

This means that you can enter different parameters in the blocks on the right, as shown in the picture. By the example of this program, the cat starts to run when clicking on "Start".

Python

Another program pre-installed on the Raspberry Pi is called Thonny. Thonny is a text-based programming tool that lets you develop Python programs and run them on the Raspberry Pi instantly. Thonny can be found in the Raspbian start menu under "Development".

So much for the pre-installed software on the Raspberry Pi. As you can already see, Raspbian is a normal operating system. As mentioned before, it is based on Debian Linux.

Therefore it is also possible to run normal programs on it. You will notice at the first start of the whole thing also works very fast. Just because the board is so small, it doesn't mean that programs or the operating system don't react so fast.

Would you like to watch this book chapter as a video? Then log into the access area at www.raspi-config.com/amazon now. You can find the access data on the last page.

8. Download the Operating System

For this chapter we will deal with the setup and installation of the Raspberry Pi. First you have to download the operating system (Raspbian). You can find it on the official website raspberrypi.org under "Downloads". I will explain the different versions to you briefly, so that you know with which version you can work best.

NOOBS

One way to set up Raspberry Pi is the NOOBS installation program. This is not your own operating system. It is just a helpful graphical interface, which is very well suited for setting up Raspberry Pi as a beginner. With NOOBS you can install different versions of Raspberry Pi, but also other operating systems can be downloaded and installed easily via NOOBS. This is the easiest way to set up the Raspberry Pi.

Image with Desktop and recommended Software

Another image is 'Raspbian Buster with desktop and recommended software', which you can also find on the download website. Raspbian Buster is the current version of the Raspbian operating system as of July 2019. And 'with desktop' means the operating system is installed with a graphical, activated user interface. Some other programs are pre-installed directly. So this is the variant that should be considered as a beginner.

Image with Desktop without Software

Then there is the variant 'Raspbian Buster with desktop'. This is the same image like above, but only that the recommended software is not pre-installed here, but it has to be installed separately.

Image without Desktop and Software

'Raspbian Buster Lite' is a minimal version of Raspbian. This version is therefore also suitable for low power devices like the Raspberry Pi Zero. This version does not have an activated graphical user interface. The operating system must therefore be operated via the command line. Here, too, no recommended software is pre-installed, but must also be installed via the command line.

Image for installation on your PC

Then there is the version 'Debian Buster with Raspberry Pi Desktop' on the Raspberry Pi website. This is a version that you can install on your laptop, virtual machine or PC to get a simple feeling for Raspbian. This version is not suitable for our purposes. We want to install the operating system directly on the Raspberry Pi.

More Operating System Images

You can download more images from the Raspberry Pi download page. These are special versions, among others an "Internet of Things" version of Windows 10 or an Ubuntu version. These are special images again, but we won't deal with that further in this book. We will deal with NOOBS and how to set up the Raspberry Pi.

You can of course also use the Raspbian version of your choice. The Lite version is not necessarily the best choice to start now. You might only need this version if you already have a pre-programmed or pre-developed solution and want to run it without a user interface. Then you don't need to install the whole system with user interface later. So it would be an option for later.

Would you like to watch this book chapter as a video? Then log into the access area at www.raspi-config.com/amazon now. You can find the access data on the last page.

9. Installation of the OS with Etcher (PC+Mac)

For this chapter I'll show you how you can use Etcher (www.balena.io/etcher/) for PC and MAC. It is easy to write the operating system for the Raspberry Pi to an SD card and you will have the SD card ready for the Raspberry Pi in a few minutes.

It's important to know that Etcher only works with the Raspbian operating system or other operating systems and not with NOOBS. NOOBS have to be installed in a different way. But I'll show you this separately in the next chapter.

To work with Etcher, you need an image from the Raspberry Pi download page, which I already introduced to you. Here you simply choose an image. I use the image 'Rasbian Buster with desktop and recommended software' and install it on my SD card.

Etcher's window is very simple and it's the only window this program has at all. So the first step is to choose an image.

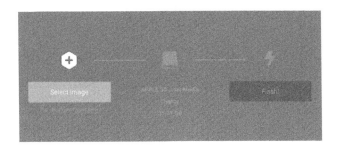

Select the storage location and then click on 'Flash!' as shown here. After that the whole image will be written to the SD card.

As soon as the writing process in Etcher is finished, it will take a moment. The SD card is ready and can be inserted into the Raspberry Pi. Now the Raspberry Pi can be connected to the power supply and started.

Would you like to watch this chapter of the book as a video? Then log into the access area at www.raspi-config.com/amazon now. You can find the access data on the last page.

10. Installation with NOOBS

After I showed you in the previous chapter how to write the operating system to an SD card with Etcher, I now want to explain to you how to install NOOBS.

As mentioned before, NOOBS is an installation program that allows you to easily install multiple operating systems on the Raspberry Pi. However, NOOBS is not installed with Etcher on the SD card. To install NOOBS on the SD card, you don't really need to do much.

There is only this one ZIP folder that can be downloaded from the Raspberry Pi website. Just unzip it as usual. Then go to the unzipped folder with all the files. All you have to do is drag and drop these files onto the SD card. That takes a little while and is almost 1.8 gigabytes of data.

Once that's done, you can slide the SD card directly into the Raspberry Pi and turn it on. Now the Raspberry Pi is ready. Just plug in a mouse, keyboard, and monitor. Then all you have to do is connect the Raspberry Pi to the power supply. You will then see the following NOOBS initial screen.

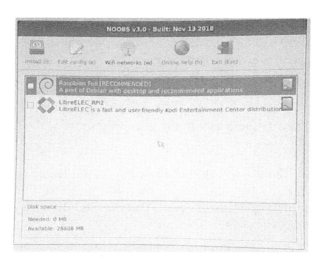

That means the Raspberry Pi will already start booting. Now you already have the graphical interface at your disposal. Next you will see NOOBS making some preparations. Now you have the possibility to choose between two operating systems.

You can also change the language to German at the bottom of the screen. After that the keyboard layout will be changed automatically. Now we want to install Raspbian. To do this, select the first item as shown in the picture above and then click on Install. Before you do that, there is still the possibility to set WLAN networks in this window.

There is an advantage to this, if you connect to a WLAN, you get even more choices offered by operating systems. But for simplicity, we only want to install Raspbian. After clicking on install the installation will start. You will then be informed that all operating systems that are already installed on the SD card will be overwritten. Since you only have one operating system on it, it doesn't matter.

So click "yes" and the installation begins. The installation is going takes its time. When the Raspberry Pi is finished, it restarts automatically and you can start using the Raspberry Pi.

Would you like to watch this book chapter as a video? Then log into the access area at www.raspi-config.com/amazon now. You can find the access data on the last page.

11. Setup with a Monitor

Next in this chapter, I would like to show you how to do the initial setup with the help of a monitor. Following in the next chapter I will explain how to do the initial setup WITHOUT using a monitor.

First Boot

You should now have a monitor connected and a message on the screen that the operating system has been successfully installed. Confirm with "ok" and Raspberry Pi will restart. You should now see the boot process. The first time you do this, it will go through everything. After that, the start screen appears. As you can see now, there is a message that the Raspberry Pi has been set up successfully. You will then be guided through a few more keyboard settings, general settings etc.

Set the User und Password

As a previous example mentioned before, I have noted that the Raspberry Pi is in Germany. Also German should be set as the language and the time zone is Berlin. If not, you can set it to your preferred country/ time-zone. Next comes the message that the default user is 'pi'. The default password is 'raspberry'. You can change that now if you want.

WLAN-Configuration

Now you can set up a WLAN and it's best to do so. After the Raspberry Pi has connected to the WLAN, you will be asked to do a software update. To do this, click 'Next'. The Raspberry Pi is already set up.

Would you like to watch this book chapter as a video? Then log into the access area at www.raspi-config.com/amazon now. You can find the access data on the last page.

12. Setup without a Monitor

As previously mentioned, I would like to show you how to set up the Raspberry Pi without a monitor. Sometimes you don't necessarily have a keyboard, mouse and monitor at your disposal.

In this case, there is also a way to set up the Raspberry Pi completely from remote. The advantage of this is that you learn how to work with the terminal commands on the Raspberry Pi at the same time. Here's a note that you can only set up the Raspberry Pi without a monitor if you don't use NOOBS. Just as side note, NOOBS was the graphical interface for the Raspberry Pi installation, we discussed in chapter 10.

Download the Image

So the next step is to download an image of your choice from the Raspberry Pi website. The image can contain a graphical interface such as "Raspbian Buster with Desktop". After downloading it, use Etcher again to write the operating system to the SD card as described in chapter 9. After writing with Etcher you will find a lot of files on your SD card.

Activate SSH

To access the Raspberry Pi remotely from your home network without using a monitor, SSH must be enabled. SSH is an access or a way to access devices and execute commands. To enable SSH access, you need to create a file on the /boot partition of your SD card that simply has the file name "ssh".

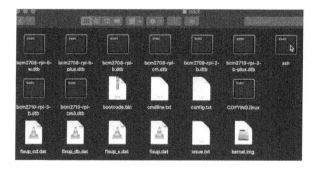

The best way to do this is to insert your SD card on your Mac, then navigate to /boot using the Finder and duplicate any file with CMD + D there. Then rename this file to "ssh".

With Windows you proceed similarly and plug your SD card into the computer. Then go to the Windows Explorer on /boot and create a new empty file with a right click + New - text file and give it the name "ssh". The file extension .txt will be deleted during renaming.

If you have problems with this, you can of course also use a very simple text editor. The only important thing is that this "ssh" file in /boot must not have an extension. Sometimes the files get the txt extension automatically. Then the access to the Raspberry Pi later via SSH will not work.

This activates SSH access on the Raspberry Pi. The only thing that needs to be considered now is to use the Raspberry Pi, you have to connect the Raspberry once via LAN to your router. Once you have done this, you can continue.

Find the IP-Address

Once you have connected the Raspberry Pi to the LAN port of your router and the power, you need to find out the IP address of the Raspberry Pi on the network. If you know how to do this on your router, like through via the web interface, you can do it on the variant.

If you don't know the IP address, you can use freeware. For the Mac, this is the LanScan software. You can find it on the Mac in the Mac App Store via the search bar. If you have a Windows PC, you can use the Freeware Advanced IP Scanner. (www.advanced-ip-scanner.com/de)

For the LanScan, the Windows program Advanced IP Scanner works the same way. Just click on "Start LanScan" and all devices in your network that are connected to the router will be listed.

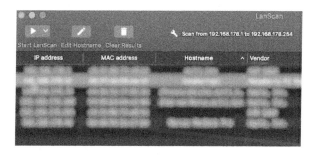

In this list, you will find Raspberry Pi. You can find it under Hostname. But even more important is the IP address of the Raspberry Pi's. Now you have to control this IP address via the terminal on the Mac or via PuTTY (putty.org) on Windows. This will access the SSH access of the Raspberry Pis.

Access over the Terminal

For this you use the command 'ssh pi@ip-adresse'. The username is 'pi' by default. Then press "Enter", so now you just have to enter the password 'raspberry' followed by Enter. And you are already logged in to the Raspberry. Bravo!

Now you can make the first settings. For this you type the command 'sudo raspi-config', because you have to execute the command as super-user (sudo) with all permissions. Now you can have a look around the following screen. You don't have to change your password now. The first thing to change is 'Configuring Locales'. These local settings are so important because they also set the 'Wi-fi Country' setting. There you have to select the country Germany or your preferred country, otherwise the WLAN cannot be activated.

Country Settings

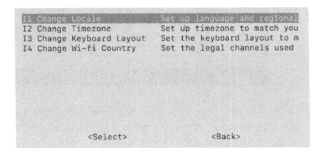

Then you get the success message and confirm it with Enter. Now you can go through all the other settings again if you want to have a look around.

VNC Remote Access

There are boot options that you can select, or should I start with the graphical user interface or with the command line? But it's best not to do that now. Where you should set something now, are the "Interfacing Options". There you will find the item VNC. VNC is a server that allows you to access the graphical interface of the Raspberry Pi's without a monitor.

VNC should be enabled under "Interfacing Options". There are other settings, but we won't go through them now. Now go back to the beginning with ESC and select 'finish'. You have now done all the basic settings.

Remote Control with RealVNC Viewer

To access the graphical interface of the Raspberry Pi's now, you can download the RealVNC program. The program is free and can be downloaded for Mac and PC from realvnc.com/en/connect/download/viewer/.

In RealVNC, enter the IP address of the Raspberry Pi. This will open a login window. You have to confirm this once with "Allow". After that, you can login to the graphical user interface with the user 'pi' and the password 'raspberry'. From now on you can use the graphical user interface of the Raspberry Pi as if you had connected a monitor.

Complete the Setup

From now on, the setup works the same as if you connected a monitor. There is the notice that it's a security risk if the username and password are not changed. However it is fine for now, since you're only making Raspberry Pi available on your network.

It will go through the steps in the user interface where you can choose to download updates. The procedure is the same as the setup with a monitor from chapter 11.

Would you like to watch this book chapter as a video? Then log into the access area at www.raspi-config.com/amazon now. You can find the access data on the last page.

13. Backup & Restore (SD-Card)

In this chapter I will explain how to create a backup from the SD card and how to restore it, if necessary.

For Mac – Apple Pi Baker

If you have a PC, you can use the free program Win32 Disk Imager (sourceforge.net/projects/win32diskimager/). If you have a Mac, you can use the Apple Pi Baker application for free (tweaking4all.com/software/macosx-software/macosx-apple-pi-baker/).

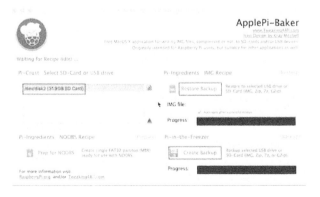

The interface is designed very simply. First you select the appropriate SD card, and then click on "Start backup". When restoring an SD card, select the appropriate backup image that has been written to a file to be written back to the card.

For PC – Win 32 Disk Imager

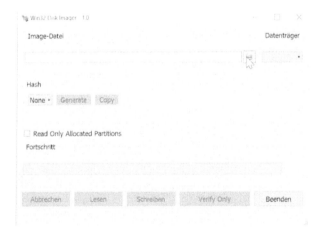

Win32 Disk Imager works very similarly. You can select a file or create an image file to back up the SD card. Then select the appropriate disk and choose either "Read" to backup or "Write" to restore the backup. That was it already.

Would you like to watch this book chapter as a video? Then log into the access area at www.raspi-config.com/amazon now. You can find the access data on the last page.

14. MicroSD Card deletion

For this chapter, I'll explain how to delete the SD card correctly. The SD Memory Card Formatter program from the official SD Association, which also developed the SD card standard, is recommended for this. You can download the program at the following URL: www.sdcard.org/downloads/formatter/

After the installation you will see the following window, which is also the only window of the program. At this point you might want to note that the window looks exactly the same for Mac and Windows.

At the top you have the option to select an SD card. Below you will find some information about the card. Further down it will be interesting, because there are the variants 'Quick format' and 'Overwrite format'. With the "Overwrite format" variant, some additional parameters on the SD card memory are overwritten.

However, it is sufficient if you use the "Quick format" variant. Then give the SD card a name and start the formatting process with the button "Format". After that you will be asked if you really want to do this, because this process irrevocably deletes all data.

After you have confirmed this, the formatting process begins. This process will then be completed very quickly. Soon after, you will get a success message, which you can simply confirm. And already the whole thing is finished.

This process is particularly worthwhile if you are using an SD card from a camera or mobile phone, like for example, to use it for the Raspberry Pi. But even if you bought a new SD card, you can still reformat it. It doesn't hurt or change anything in the end.

Would you like to watch this book chapter as a video? Then log into the access area at www.raspi-config.com/amazon now. You can find the access data on the last page.

15. Software Projects

In the next few chapters I would like to implement several projects together with you. These are all software-based projects. That means you only need your Raspberry Pi and no other sensors.

Pi-Hole

What I would to specifically go over with you in the next chapters are the projects of a network-wide advertising blocker (Pi-Hole). Over which you can later run your Internet traffic to remove advertisements and trackers while surfing the Internet.

Homebridge

The second project we are implementing together is the Homebridge project. It allows you to connect multiple devices to Apple's HomeKit that are not actually compatible with HomeKit. This will save you a lot of money, because you don't have to buy certified devices like heating thermostats.

Webmin

The third project is called Webmin, where we will install a system administration interface for the Raspberry Pi. This project is especially recommended because it will make your daily work with the Raspberry Pi much easier. This will allow you to control the entire system from an easy-to-use interface and perform many tasks that would otherwise only be possible from the command line.

As I said, for all these projects you don't need any additional sensors. All you need is your Raspberry Pi.

Would you like to watch this book chapter as a video? Then log into the access area at www.raspi-config.com/amazon now. You can find the access data on the last page.

16. Project: Pi-Hole

Now, I'll show you how to install the network-wide ad blocker called Pi-Hole on the Raspberry Pi.

I will do it all from the terminal on the Raspberry Pi. The whole thing also works, if you log in remotely via SSH with "ssh pi@ip-adresse" via PuTTy on your Raspberry Pi. The steps remain the same.

First of all we want to update the Raspberry Pi and download the updates. To do this, enter the command 'sudo apt - get update' followed by Enter. This will take a little while. When this is done, run the command 'sudo apt - get upgrade' to install the new versions of the software.

Now we want to download Pi-hole. For this we give this command on the terminal 'curl - sSL https://install.pi-hole.net | bash'. This will download the script behind this address and the Bash command will execute this script.

Now all packages for Pi-Hole will be installed automatically. It even has a nice graphical interface. Then you will be guided through the installations. Confirm all further queries with Enter to proceed to the actual installation. Now the message appears that Pi-Hole is free and Open Source.

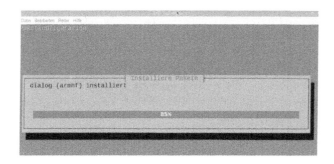

Then the message appears that the Raspberry Pi needs a static IP address. Now it is usually the case that routers assign new IP addresses to devices from time to time. You should find this in your router settings, otherwise just google your router model and look for static IP addresses.

Now you have to choose what you want the network traffic to run over, either via the Ethernet port, which has the internal name eth0, or via the WLAN port wlan0. Personally, I have connected my Raspberry Pi via WLAN, so I choose wlan0. Now I want to select a DNS provider, which will be used for DNS requests later. You should be aware that every DNS request always transmits certain data and that this data is visible at the provider.

This means that you can select one of the known DNS providers here. One of your options is to select a "Custom" DNS server. The DNS server, I chose is addressed as 194.150.168.168. Behind this IP address is a DNS server from the Chaos Computer Club, which anonymizes all DNS requests.

You can also choose one of the default DNS servers. Now you can confirm with Enter. Now you will be asked again, are the IP addresses correct? Confirm with "Yes". Now so-called blacklists are to be downloaded, which can recognize the advertisement in the Internet traffic immediately. That is, they are lists of addresses that typically play advertising.

The best thing is to simply download all the lists. You can choose later if you want to deselect some of them again. Now there is the question of which advertising requests to block over, either over IPv4 or over IPv6. Choose IPv4 and deselect the IPv6 version. Usually all IP addresses are running on version 4. After that you will be asked again if these network settings are correct. Then the IP address of the Raspberry Pi's should be recognized correctly. You press this again with Ok. Now comes a hint. Confirm this with Ok.

In the next step you will be asked if you want to call the admin interface via the browser and if you want to install it. Confirm this with, as this is a practical thing and a good way to control Pi-Hole very easily. And now we log the queries too, then you always have a complete overview of how much advertising was filtered out. But you can turn that off later.

Now we can decide which mode we want to set for privacy and data protection. Here you can also select everything to have an overview of what the pi-hole does in particular. Otherwise, that's it with the whole installation. The complete setup is now complete. Below is the password you need to use to log in to the web interface. It is best to write down the password briefly or copy it into a text file.

The installation is now complete. You can now access the Raspberry Pi or Pi-Hole web interface via your browser. Simply enter the IP address of the Raspberry Pi in your browser, followed by /admin. The following web interface will open.

Now we want to log in to this web interface. Therefore we go to the Login page and enter the password that was shown to you at the end of the installation. Now you have access to all settings, edit white lists, and so on.

Now we have to make sure that we switch the Raspberry Pi between every computer, tablet and smartphone so that every DNS request is filtered and advertising is blocked. To do this, log into your router and reset the DNS address. The new DNS address in your router must be rewritten to the IP address of your Raspberry Pi's, so that all DNS requests from the router can first be filtered via Raspberry Pi's servers. You can find out how to change the DNS settings on your router in the manual of your router. Before you change the DNS settings, call up a page of your choice with lots of advertisements to compare it as soon as Pi-Hole is activated.

When this is done, we want to see Pi-Hole in action. To do this, you can call up the T-Online page, because it has a lot of advertising. Do you see the difference? If I reload the page, the web traffic should now run through the Raspberry Pi. And as you can see, the advertising has disappeared. That is, Pi-hole has struck and removed the advertising.

Would you like to watch this book chapter as a video? Then log into the access area at www.raspi-config.com/amazon now. You can find the access data on the last page.

17. Project: Homebridge

In this chapter, I would like to introduce you to the project "Homebridge". Homebridge is a kind of Smart Home central, with which you can connect devices with Apple's HomeKit.

You can find out how to install this application step-by-step in the instructions at http://www.smartapfel.de/homebridge/ I will now show you how to set up Homebridge more precisely. After the installation you should be able to open this login window by entering the IP address of your Raspberry Pi in the browser of your choice and writing :8080 behind it.

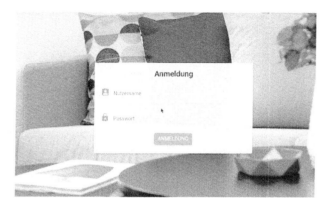

You can log in with the **username admin** and the **password admin**. Through this you are already in the web interface to configure the whole thing now.

You can then use your iOS or Apple device to scan the displayed QR code and add the configured devices to HomeKit. In this example, we want to add a "Fake Bulb" device, which is a virtual bulb that can be controlled by HomeKit.

To do this go to the menu under "Plugins" and install 'Fake RGB Bulb plugin for homebridge' via the NPM link. If that was successful, then you are already a good step further. Now we open the configuration file in the menu "Config" and find the item 'Accessories', where we have to insert the code snippet from the NPM page. You should see the code 'Fake-RGB'. This is the name of the accessory.

Homebridge Config Editor

```
 5      "port": 51826,
 6      "pin": "031-45-154"
 7    },
 8    "description": "Home Smart Home",
 9    "platforms": [
10      {
11        "platform": "config",
12        "name": "Config",
13        "port": 8080,
14        "auth": "form",
15        "theme": "red",
16        "restart": "sudo -n systemctl restart homebridge",
17        "temp": "/sys/class/thermal/thermal_zone0/temp",
18        "sudo": true,
19        "log": {
20          "method": "systemd",
21          "service": "homebridge"
22        }
23      }
24    ],
25    "accessories": [{
26      "accessory": "Fake-RGB",
27      "name": "Birne 1"
28    },
29    {
30      "accessory": "Fake-RGB",
31      "name": "Birne 2"
32    }]
33  }
```

And now we can give this whole thing a name. I'm going to call this 'Lamp 1'. And if we put a comma behind it, then we can insert the whole thing again and have immediately created the second bulb. Then save and "Config successfully saved" appears. After restarting the Homebridge, we can now test our two fake pears, switch them on once and switch them off again.

You can now make the complete settings for the pears. The bulbs can be turned on and dimmed etc. The good thing about Homebridge is that you can use plugins to add many different devices like the Philipps Hue lamps or connect the whole thing to Amazon's Alexa.

There are some great examples of how you can extend Homebridge here, but now we've installed two fake bulbs to play around with. If we now connect Homebridge to our iOS device, then we can control these virtual bulbs directly from the iPhone, iPad or Mac. Of course, this doesn't do much with virtual devices, but to get a feeling I've shown you the possibilities you have with additional accessories to automate your home at a reasonable price.

Would you like to watch this book chapter as a video? Then log into the access area at www.raspi-config.com/amazon now. You can find the access data on the last page.

18. Project: Webmin

Now I would like to show you the Webmin interface. How to install Webmin can be found in this well done guide: https://timobihlmaier.de/webmin-als-webinterface-auf-dem-raspberry-pi-installieren/

Webmin is an interface that allows you to easily manage the Raspberry Pi system and perform many tasks that would otherwise have to be performed from the terminal, i.e. from the command line.

Webmin is simply a very practical way to make many settings on the Raspberry Pi. I have installed Webmin and log in normally with my login data.

If you have Webmin installed, you can access it by typing the IP address of your Raspberry Pi into your browser, followed by a colon and the number 10000. After that you will see this interface.

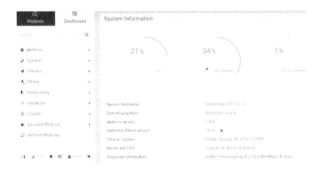

Now you can see all the data about your Raspberry Pi, from your current load and so on. I have 21 percent CPU usage at the moment. Otherwise we can see the memory usage and so on. So there is a lot of data to discover about your Raspberry Pi.

You can now make many different settings for the Raspberry Pi on the interface. One possibility is that you can install new programs, which would otherwise be cumbersome to install from the command line.

Now I look under the tab "System" -> "Software Packages" whether I already installed the Apache TP Server? No, I don't have it yet. Then I would install Apache as a test. If you want to do this, go to 'Package from APT' and search for the word "Apache".

Then you get an overview of the results and can install "Apache 2" by pressing a button. That's how easy it is to install packages. You can also easily access the system logs via Webmin or create and add new users. Webmin is a very practical interface that will make it much easier for you to manage your Raspberry Pi.

Would you like to watch this book chapter as a video? Then log in to the access area at www.raspi-config.com/amazon now. You can find the access data on the last page.

19. Project: RetroPi + KODI

Now, I want to show you how to install RetroPie. With RetroPie you can turn your Raspberry Pi into a kind of classic game console with which you can play old games like Amiga 500, Nintendo64, or Playstation 1 flawlessly.

You can download RetroPie on the website retropie.org.uk/download/. There are two different versions, one for the Raspberry Pi version 0/1 and one for the Raspberry Pi 2 and 3. Downloading takes a moment because the file is very large.

Once you have downloaded the image, you can write it to the SD card using Etcher and then start the Raspberry Pi. After the installation on the SD card we have to start the configuration. For the configuration at this point, it makes sense to buy a gamepad first. For example this wireless gamepad from GameSir: https://amzn.to/2IGFf94

With such a gamepad you can make the setup much easier. When you boot RetroPi for the first time, you will notice that the configuration is not designed to be done with a keyboard, but with a gamepad. You can also use a Plastation 3 or an Xbox360 controller for configuration if you have it at hand.

When booting it for the first time, you have to hold a button on the gamepad to start the setup. The first step is to assign the control buttons that you will find on the gamepad. Once you've finished configuring the control buttons, you'll be taken to the RetroPie main menu. You can now continue with the configuration here.

We can now access the RetroPi menu. Here you will find all the necessary settings, including the 'RASPI-CONFIG' item, where we can call up the Raspberry Pi settings and make familiar settings. Now we should set up a WiFi network first, because KODI will be downloaded later. KODI is a Smart-TV extension and for this we need an internet connection.

In order to set up the Wifi connection, we first have to set up our WiFi country settings. This means that we determine in which country we are currently using. This is to assure that the WiFi connection and the communication between Raspberry Pi and the router works properly. For this we have to go to the normal settings of Raspberry Pi (raspi-config) and look for the "localization settings" where we set the WiFi country.

In the list below you can find Germany/ Deutschland. Now you can already go out of the settings again. Now we connect to the WiFi network. When you are connected, it goes back to the settings of RetroPie.

Now we can set up Kodi. Therefore we have to go into the setup of RetroPie. The setup can also be found in the configuration and here we first have to update the RetroPie setup script, so first download a new version.

Then we can install KODI. To do this, select the menu item 'Manage packages' and you will find a whole list of packages under 'Manage optional packages', which you can download and install.

Now you have to scroll a bit to point 312, where we see 'kodi' and can start the installation with "Enter". After the installation is finished, you will see the window that shows you how to edit the packages.

There we can go out, because all packages have been installed. Now we should do a reboot and after that we can test KODI right away.

At the moment RetroPie still starts first. But we want to set this up so that Kodi starts first and you can access RetroPie from there. Now we see the possibility to switch between RetroPie, the configuration, and the ports. It is important to note that the ports are now KODI.

When you are going start this, it will take a short moment as we see KODI start.

Back in the RetroPie interface we can now go back to the configuration and find under RetroPie Setup the possibility to change the auto-start function. There you can now choose whether Emulation Station (RetroPie) or KODI should boot at startup. Here you choose 'Start Kodi at boot'. Now restart again and KODI should start first.

If you click in KODI at the top on the switch off symbol and then 'Exit', you come back again to the RetroPie surface and thus again into the game console. What's missing now, of course, are the games. You don't get any games with RetroPie, you have to install them yourself. On the site Mamedev.org you can also find free games, which you can download and use.

Otherwise you need the original game license, which you have to buy. Then you can also play the games on RetroPie. Of course, it is recommended to use a real gamepad. At this point the restriction has to be mentioned. RetroPi is not a full game console. You can mainly play very old games up to Playstation 1. So RetroPi is a very nice gimmick. At the same time you have also integrated an entertainment center and all that on the small Raspberry Pi. Isn't that fantastic?

Would you like to watch this book chapter as a video? Then log into the access area at www.raspi-config.com/amazon now. You can find the access data on the last page.

20. Hardware Projects

This and the next three chapters will be about sensors and modules for the Raspberry Pi. In the first chapter, I have already introduced you to the SunFounder Sensor Kit with 37 parts. In this kit you'll find really everything, like buttons, LED diodes and various sensors.

I would like to explain a little bit about this sensor in the three chapters. For example, the soil moisture sensor, which can detect and measure moisture. I want to show you something about a light sensitivity sensor that can detect brightness. In addition, I want to show you how to connect an LED to the Raspberry Pi.

I will show you this with a laser beam diode, which is combined with the light sensitivity sensor to form a light barrier. And I would like to tell you a little bit more about the camera that is sold by the Raspberry Pi Foundation. With this camera you can, for example, operate a surveillance camera.

Therefore I would like to explain to you how to connect these modules to the Raspberry Pi and how to control and use them. The pins on the side of the Raspberry Pi are basic for the use of sensors and modules. There is a specific assignment plan for this. You can find it here: www.elektronik-kompendium.de/sites/raspberry-pi/1907101.htm

For example, if we have the two pins above that are responsible for the power supply and there are the ground pins with which we can intercept the returned current, i.e. ground the devices again and in a certain way decrease the return voltage. We have other pins that are there to take data. We also have pins with different voltages.

You always have to be careful, because there are some pins connected directly to the processor. If you connect something wrong, it can also cause a short circuit and theoretically dispose of the Raspberry Pi if something goes wrong... The pins on the Raspberry Pi are all numbered and have different meanings, as you can see on the assignment plan.

Now we can implement the hardware projects via the pins. In the next couple of chapters I will explain how to connect modules to the pins, how to use them, and how to control them. Once you have understood the basic principle, you can, for example, use and combine various modules from the SunFounder Kit. Click here for the SunFounder Starter Kit: https://amzn.to/2LHpnrx

Would you like to watch this book chapter as a video? Then log into the access area at www.raspi-config.com/amazon now. You can find the access data on the last page.

21. Project: Camera-Module

In this chapter, I would like to introduce the camera module for the Raspberry Pi. The camera module is officially published by the Raspberry Pi Foundation and is very easy to connect and use.

Some technical data about this camera. The camera has a total of 8 megapixels, which is quite a lot for such a simple module. The camera has a video resolution of 1080p, so it supports Full HD. There is also a camera module that has an infrared sensor and can be used at night. That brings us to the possible applications of this camera module. One possibility would be to use the camera as a surveillance camera.

There are now many projects that can be found on the Internet, with which users have built a surveillance camera with a motion sensor. Where, movements are detected on the basis of the camera image and information about intruders is provided. This is just one example of how this camera can be used. The use as a surveillance camera is certainly the most common use on the Raspberry Pi.

On the Raspberry Pi we have two connections for it, which actually look very similar. We have this flat plug at the bottom of the camera, which we simply insert into the Raspberry Pi.

We must note that we also have a connector for an LCD display that can be used with exactly the same connector. And we have the connection for the camera as shown in the picture. You can tell the difference by looking at the circuit board. Next to the connectors there is the display connector and the camera connector. With this knowledge the connection is actually quite easy. You simply take the tape or cable and plug it a little carefully into the camera connector from above.

Now I will explain how you can use the camera module. To be able to use the camera on the Raspberry Pi, we have to activate the camera module in the Raspbian operating system. Therefore we go into the terminal and type the command 'sudo raspi-config'. Under "Interfacing Options" you will find the option "Camera".

When activating you will be asked, do you want to activate the Camera Interface? Select "Yes". Then you get the message "Camera Interface is enabled". That's all we have to do, except restart Raspberry Pi.

To take a photo with the camera now, we use a very simple command and in the terminal called 'raspistill - o image.jpg' and enter a filename after the command like Image.jpg. Then press Enter and the photo will be created. You will then find the photo in your home directory.

Of course you have to say that this is not a high-end camera, even if the resolution is relatively high. We can also record a video with the Raspberry camera. For this we use the command 'raspivid - t'. And then you specify the length in milliseconds. I now enter ten thousand for ten seconds. Enter the codec in which we want to do the whole thing, with '-o video.h264', an MPEG-4 file. So the command is 'raspivid -t 10000 -o video.h264'.

You can still adjust some more, but this is only a test now. After the ten seconds we find the video again in the home directory. You can then open the video with the VLC Player. During playback you can also see that the camera is not the best. But as I said before, for a surveillance camera it is worthwhile to set up plus simple and cheap.

Would you like to watch this book chapter as a video? Then log into the access area at www.raspi-config.com/amazon now. You can find the access data on the last page.

22. Project: Humidity Sensor

Now in this chapter, I would like to explain how you can use a soil moisture sensor on the Raspberry Pi. I'll explain how to connect it and how to control and read it with the Raspberry Pi.

To connect the soil moisture sensor to the Raspberry Pi, we need a total of five and a translation chip that makes the data readable.

First I connect two cables to the soil moisture sensor. These are simply plugged on as shown here. Then I connect the other end to the chip. So the sensor is already connected to the translation chip.

Now three more cables follow, which we find on the back of the translation chip. One is VCC, GND, DO and AO. VCC is the power connector. GND is the ground and DO is the digital output, AO is the analog output. For a better understanding of the cable connections I recommend you to watch the video in the login area at www.raspi-config.com/amazon now.

We now need the digital output (DO). I close the three cables directly next to each other and if you turn the chip over, the right pin remains free. Now we take the end of the cables and plug them into the Raspberry Pi. At the top right, I connect the first pin, because this is the 3.3 Volt connector. We will need this later for the translation chip or sensor.

We then connect the Ground to the Raspberry Pi and directly underneath the DO, the cable for the digital output. We connect the sensor to it and now we need a Python script to get the data. You can turn on the Raspberry Pi and at this point we'd like to add a few words; you will find a pin assignment plan on various pages on the Internet. Link to the assignment plan: www.elektronik-kompendium.de/sites/raspberry-pi/1907101.htm

On the assignment plan you can see again how the pins on the Raspberry Pi are assigned. So the power is connected at the top and next to it is the VCC connector with the 3.3 Volt voltage. We have them at the fifth pin from above the ground connection, and the GND. Directly below at pin number 17 we have the data, which we have to read out there now.

To read the data I have prepared a script, which you can download from www.raspi-config.com/amazon. The script is kept relatively simple and to the point with a short yet brief explanation. At the top, a library is embedded, which allows to access the GPIO pins.

Then there is a time library that allows you to set a timer. We'll soon see what this is important for. And then I added a callback function that is always called when a new value is measured at the sensor. Instead, the output "No water detected" appears when the LED is off. And if the LED is on, then water was detected at the sensor. So then 'Water detected' is output. Then we set the mode from which we pass the numbering. Through this, we define the Chanel of pin 17, which we have just seen on the allocation plan and pick up the data there.

Then a few functions and the timer follow in the script. This means, pin 17 is continuously monitored and if a new measured value is measured, then the callback function is executed. Now let's have a look at the script in action.

To test the script I use a cup with water into which I will carefully dip the sensor 2x and take it out again. Now you see the output of the script that monitors the sensor.

What can you use it for now? One possibility would be to link this to an e-mail output and thus monitor your favorite flower or flower pot to see whether the potting soil is still moist enough. The same applies of course to the lawn in the garden. You can use this soil moisture sensor very well for this.

By the way, there are also soil moisture sensors with which you can measure much more filigree. These sensors output the values even more filigree. This sensor in the example at least detects whether it is damp or not.

Would you like to watch this book chapter as a video? Then log into the access area at www.raspi-config.com/amazon now. You can find the access data on the last page.

23. Project: Light Sensor

For this chapter, I would like to introduce you to the light sensitivity module and show you how it works. The sensitivity module consists of only one chip. We want to connect the sensitivity sensor to the Raspberry Pi. For this we need three connecting cables VCC, GND, and DO and nothing more.

Once you have the connecting cables, you can just connect the power supply, the ground, and the digital output together for the data. After that you can connect the Raspberry Pi to the power supply and let's see the module in action.

For the light sensitivity module, I wrote a Python script which reads the data at PIN 21 of the Raspberry Pi and looks what value it has. You can find the script in the login area at www.raspi-config.com/amazon . If the script has the value 0, then the light is on. If it has the value 1, then the light is off.

This script runs all the time on the Raspberry Pi and monitors whether there is a change in the value of PIN 21. On one side of the module we have the power LED, which simply indicates that the module is powered. The other is a kind of control diode where you can see the state that is being transmitted.

When running the script over Thonny (chapter 26) you can see the output of the script in the lower half of the screen.

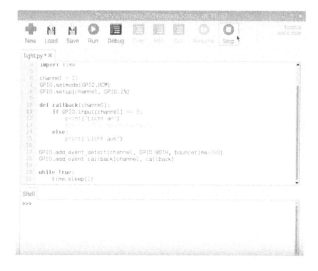

I'm going to turn the lights on and off right now. The connected sensor now detects whether the light is on or off and emits it accordingly in the lower area of Thonny. This is a practical option if you have lights that are not internet enabled. Then you can easily check it. But there are also many other ways to use this module in your everyday and professional life.

```
Shell
>>> %Run light.py
  Licht aus
  Licht an
```

Would you like to watch this book chapter as a video? Then log in to the access area at www.raspi-config.com/amazon now. You can find the access data on the last page.

24. Project: Laser Module

For this chapter, I would like to show you another use for the light sensitivity sensor from the previous chapter. This time in combination with the laser beam module.

I assembled the construction from both modules to a light barrier. On one side of the wooden rod there is the laser diode, which is directed to the light sensitivity sensor on the other side. The idea is that the light sensitivity sensor detects when someone passes through the light barrier.

If the connection between the two sensors is interrupted and a change in brightness is detected, it should be displayed on the screen. This is a useful function to display different states or to build light control modes.

The best way is to watch the video at www.raspi-config.com/amazon to better understand how to connect the cables. As you can see in the picture, we have attached the light sensitivity sensor to the wooden pole.

Then we attached the emitting diode to the wooden rod. The LED has two cables that have to be connected to the Raspberry Pi. One cable for the power supply and one cable for the ground connection. Now you have to connect these two cables, and the 3 Volt (not 5 Volt), then the ground for the light emitting diode. If you connect the Raspberry Pi to the power supply, the LED would be switched on, because the power pins have a continuous power supply.

Now let's have a look at the light barrier in action. For this, I use the Python script again, which I already used for the light sensitivity sensor. You can download the script at www.raspi-config.com/amazon. Because from the light sensitivity sensor we read the data again.

Of course, this is only set up at a very short distance. Purely theoretically you could operate a light barrier with the laser across a room or over a distance of one meter or more. However, the further away you get, the harder it will be to hit the small sensor on the module.

You will see either two control LEDs light up. This means that the sensor is currently seeing light and the light barrier is not interrupted. Another very important hint at this point. NEVER look directly into the light of the laser diode!

Now I hold such a wooden stick between the light barrier in my construction. Now you see the output of the Python script that the whole thing was recognized. When I go up again with the wooden stick, then the light at the sensor is there again. So you could build a light barrier with this laser diode in combination with the light sensitivity sensor. This is just another example for the use of modules on the Raspberry Pi. Do you now have your own ideas about what you want to do with them?

Would you like to watch this book chapter as a video? Then log into the access area at www.raspi-config.com/amazon now. You can find the access data on the last page.

25. Video: Programming with Scratch

You can only view this lesson in the online section. So log in to the access area at www.raspi-config.com/amazon now. You can find the access data on the last page.

26. Video: Programming with Thonny

You can only view this lesson in the online section. So log in to the access area at www.raspi-config.com/amazon now. You can find the access data on the last page.

27. 100 Quiz-Questions

To train your knowledge from this book you can have fun with some quiz questions now. In the next pages I will ask you over 100 quiz questions we have discussed in the sections before. You will find the right answers on the last pages of this book for your confirmation.

Lesson 1. What is a Raspberry Pi?

1. Who developed the Raspberry Pi?
    1. Cherry Pi Foundation in Thailand
    2. Raspberry Pi Foundation in England (UK)
    3. Berry Pi Foundation in Germany

2. When did the first Raspberry Pi come onto the market?
    1. 2010
    2. 2011
    3. 2012

3. How many Raspberry Pi's were sold worldwide by the end of 2017?
    1. 17 Million pieces
    2. 250.000 pieces
    3. 1ß pieces

4. What is so special about the Raspberry Pi computer?
    1. It's size in credit card format.
    2. It can fly independently.
    3. It is as powerful as current super computers.

5. What is the goal of the Raspberry Pi Foundation?
    1. To bake the best raspberry cake. ;-)
    2. To introduce young people and pupils to programming.
    3. To develop the fastest computer.

Lesson 2: Which exciting Raspberry Pi projects exist?

1. Which projects were presented?
    1. LibreELEC, HomeBridge, MagicMirror, Pi-Hole, RetroPi
    2. I can't remember. ;-)

3. Magic Hole, HomeELEC, LibreMirror

2. What can you do with Pi-Hole?
    1. Organize dates
    2. Filter out advertising
    3. Call a friend

3. What can you do with KODI?
    1. Run a multimedia center, listen to internet radio, watch movies, etc.
    2. Write documents.
    3. Cut videos like a pro.

4. What can you do with HomeBridge?
    1. I don't know. ;-)
    2. Home automation such as controlling lamps from a mobile phone.
    3. Play Playstation 4 games.

Lesson 3. Which exciting Raspberry Pi projects exist?

1. Which projects were presented in this course?
    1. LibreELEC, HomeBridge, MagicMirror, Pi-Hole, RetroPi
    2. I can't remember. ;-)
    3. Magic Hole, HomeELEC, LibreMirror

2. What can you do with Pi-Hole?
    1. Organize dates

2. Filter out advertising
   3. Call a friend

3. What can you do with KODI?
   1. Run a multimedia center, listen to internet radio, watch movies, etc.
   2. Write documents.
   3. Cut videos like a pro.

4. What can you do with HomeBridge?
   1. Run a multimedia center, listen to internet radio, watch movies, etc.
   2. Write documents.
   3. Cut videos like a pro.

Lesson 4: Which Raspberry Pi models are available and which one is the right for me?

1. What is the latest Raspberry Pi version?
   1. Raspberry Pi 3B+
   2. Raspberry Pi 3B
   3. Raspberry Pi 3

2. How much memory does the Raspberry Pi 3B+ have?
   1. 3GB Arbeitsspeicher
   2. 1GB Arbeitsspeicher
   3. 4GB Arbeitsspeicher

3. Has the Raspberry Pi 3B+ already WIFI built-in?

1. Yes.
   2. No.
   3. I don't know.

4. What is the smallest Raspberry Pi variant?
   1. Raspberry Pi 2
   2. Raspberry Pi Zero
   3. Raspberry Pi 3B+

5. Which model is recommended for this video course?
   1. Raspberry Pi 2
   2. Raspberry Pi 3B
   3. Raspberry Pi 3B+

Lesson 5: Where can I buy a Raspberry Pi + accessories?

1. What do you need in addition to the Raspberry Pi?
   1. microSD card
   2. external hard drive
   3. an additional fan.

2. What size is recommended for the microSD card?
   1. 16GB
   2. 32GB
   3. 8 GB

3. What is important, when you buy a microSD card?
   1. It should have the speed class 10.
   2. It should have the speed class 7.

3. It should have the speed class 3.

4. What is a useful accessory for the Raspberry Pi?
   1. An additional mathematical 68000 co-processor.
   2. 37 Modules and Sensors Starter Kit from Sunfounder
   3. A turbo graphics card.

5. How can you avoid "Under-Voltage" messages because of a low power supply?
   1. With the original Raspberry Pi power supply.
   2. With a normal USB cable for the power supply.
   3. By increasing the voltage.

Lesson 6: Technical data and interfaces

1. What is on the SOC "System - on -a- Chip"?
   1. All the hard disk space.
   2. Processor, main memory, graphics card
   3. Anything to do with sound.

2. At what operating temperature does the processor automatically clock down?
   1. From 20 degrees.
   2. From 40 degrees.
   3. From 70 degrees.

3. How much RAM does the Raspberry 3B+ have?
   1. 1GB of RAM.
   2. 2GB of RAM.

3. 3GB of RAM.

4. How fast is the Raspberry 3B+ graphics processor?
   1. 400 Mhz
   2. 33 Mhz
   3. 1 Ghz

5. What is so special about the 3.5mm audio connector?
   1. It is also a digital audio connection. (SPDIF)
   2. It is also a micro USB port.
   3. # It is also a composite video connector.

6. What does the chip with the raspberry symbol on it?
   1. This chip provides infrared and DAB.
   2. This chip provides Wifi and Bluetooth functionality.
   3. This chip has no function whatsoever.

7. Where is the microSD card slot located?
   1. On the left side of the Raspberry Pi 3B+.
   2. On the upper side of the Raspberry Pi 3B+.
   3. On the lower side of the Raspberry Pi 3B+.

8. How much watts does the Raspberry 3B+ consume approximately under full load?
   1. 3 watts per hour.
   2. 30 watts per hour.
   3. 300 watts per hour.

Lesson 7. What can I do with a Raspberry Pi after the first start?

1. Which software do you find pre-installed after the first start?
    1. Nothing.
    2. Libre Office Suite, Chromium web browser, small games etc.
    3. MS Office, Final Cut Pro and more.

2. What is the operating system of the Raspberry Pi?
    1. Raspbian
    2. Pi Linux
    3. AnanasOS

3. How can you open the start menu?
    1. Click on the pineapple in the upper left corner.
    2. Click on the cherry at the bottom left.
    3. By clicking on the raspberry at the top left corner.

4. Which program can be used for programming/develop on the Raspberry Pi?
    1. Scratch und Python
    2. Switch
    3. Clinch

5. Which operating system is Raspian based on?
    1. Linux (Debian)
    2. macOS

3. Microsoft Windows

Lesson 8: Downloading the operating system

1. Where can you download the Raspbian operating system for the Raspberry Pi?
    1. At www.raspberrypi.org/downloads/
    2. At www.apple.com
    3. At www.microsoft.com

2. What is NOOBS?
    1. A text-based installation program for the Raspberry Pi operating system.
    2. A graphical installation program for the Raspberry Pi operating system.
    3. A voice-controlled installation program for the Raspberry Pi operating system.

3. What includes Raspbian with desktop and recommended software?
    1. This version includes a graphical user interface and recommended software.
    2. This version includes a graphical user interface and recommended software.
    3. This version includes a graphical user interface without recommended software.

4. What is Raspbian Lite?
    1. This version does not include a graphical user interface.

2. This version includes a graphical user interface and recommended software.
3. This version includes a graphical user interface without recommended software.

5. Which operating system can be installed on the Raspberry Pi?
   1. Windows 7
   2. Ubuntu MATE
   3. macOS

Lesson 9: Installation of the operating system with Etcher

1. What can you NOT do with Etcher?
   1. Install Ubuntu.
   2. Install Raspbian.
   3. Install NOOBS.

2. What do you have to do first?
   1. Download a tutorial for Etcher.
   2. Download the operating system Raspbian.
   3. Download other software.

3. What does Etcher do with the downloaded Raspbian operating system?
   1. I don't know. ;-)
   2. It deletes the microSD card and nothing else.
   3. It writes the Raspbian operating system to the microSD card.

Lesson 10: Installation of the operating system with NOOBS

1. How do you install NOOBS on the microSD card?
    1. Just unzip the .srt folder.
    2. Unzip the NOOBS .zip file and copy the files to the microSD card.
    3. Just unzip the .zip folder with NOOBS.

2. What do you do directly after installing NOOBS?
    1. Format the microSD card again.
    2. Download NOOBS again.
    3. Insert the microSD card into the Raspberry Pi and start the Raspberry Pi.

3. What happens after starting the Raspberry Pi with the microSD card inserted?
    1. The NOOBS installation interface appears.
    2. The Raspbian surface appears.
    3. The Windows 7 installation interface appears.

4. How do you install Raspbian on the microSD card?
    1. Select "LibreELEC (recommended)" and click on "Install".
    2. With select "Ubuntu (recommended)" and click on "Install".
    3. # With select "Raspbian (recommended)" and click on "Install".

Lesson 11: Setup with a monitor

1. What do you have to configure after the first start of Raspbian?
    1. The USB settings.
    2. The WLAN settings.
    3. The Bluetooth settings.

2. What is the default user and password of Raspbian?
    1. Username: pi Password: raspberry
    2. Username: an Password: pineapple
    3. Username: ch Password: cherry

3. What should you do after the first start before you finally start?
    1. The suggested hardware update.
    2. The suggested software updates. Command: sudo apt-get upgrade & apt-get update
    3. Uninstalling the PDF Viewer.

Lesson 12: Setup WITHOUT a monitor (headless installation)

1. What do you need to activate to access the Raspberry Pi without a monitor?
    1. SSH
    2. LKM
    3. HKK

2. How do you activate SSH access?
    1. Just create a file named "lkh" on the microSD

card on the "boot" partition.
2. Simply create a file named "ssh" on the microSD card on the "boot" partition.
3. Just create a file named "mhh" on the microSD card on the "boot" partition.

3. How do you find out the IP address of your Raspberry Pi after rebooting?
1. In my router, with LANScan (Mac) or Advanced IP Scanner (PC).
2. With a search on the Internet.
3. I look at the back of my router for the IP address.

4. What command do you use to access the Raspberry via Putty or the terminal?
1. ssh <IP address> -l pi
2. ssh <IP address> -l pineapple
3. ssh <IP address> -l cherry

5. With which command can you now configure the Raspberry Pi?
1. raspiconfig
2. sudo raspi-config
3. start raspi-config

6. What should you setup first?
1. The "Locale" settings to the region DE/Germany
2. The "Locale" settings to the region FR/France

3. The "Locale" settings to the region EN/USA and then the "Wi-Fi Country" settings to EN/USA.

7. Which "Interfacing Options" should be activated to be able to access the graphical user interface of Raspbian later?
    1. VNC
    2. SPC
    3. CLI

8. How do you access the Raspbian desktop after activating VNC?
    1. Via the Unreal Viewer program.
    2. Via the RealVNC Viewer program.
    3. Via the Remote Viewer program.

Lesson 13: Backup + Restore the SD Card

1. Which application can you use to create an SD card backup with a Mac?
    1. Win 32 Disk Imager
    2. Apple Ananas Baker
    3. Apple Pi Baker

2. Which application can you use to create an SD card backup with a PC?
    1. Apple Pi Baker
    2. Win32 Disk Imager
    3. Camtasia

3. What is a backup useful for?
    1. So that the SD card does not break.
    2. If something goes wrong, I can restore the saved image with all settings immediately.
    3. I don't know.

4. Is it possible to perform a restore with both programs?
    1. Yes.
    2. No.
    3. Maybe. ;-)

Lesson 14: Formatting the micro SD card

1. Which program can you use to empty/format an SD card?
    1. SD Card Cleaner
    2. SD Card Formatter
    3. SD Card Restorer

2. Why is it sometimes useful to empty/format an SD card?
    1. To cleanly erase all data on the SD card.
    2. So that the SD card does not break.
    3. There is no real reason for this ;-)

Lesson 15: Software based Projects

1. What is "Pi Hole"?

1. An advertising blocker limited to one device.
2. A network-wide ad blocker.
3. A game on the Raspberry Pi.

2. What can you do with "Homebridge"?
    1. Connect Smarthome devices to Windows Phone.
    2. Connect Smarthome devices to Andoid Auto.
    3. Connect Smarthome devices to Apple's HomeKit.

3. What is "Webmin"?
    1. A handy user interface for system management.
    2. A practical terminal program for system administration.
    3. Practical software for creating documents.

Lesson 16: Software Project: Pi-Hole

1. What should you do before you install Pi Hole?
    1. Perform a software update with "sudo apt-get update" and "sudo apt-get upgrade" on the terminal.
    2. Open the Chrome Browser.
    3. Install Firefox Update.

2. Is "Pi-Hole" free of charge?
    1. No.
    2. Yes.
    3. I don't know. ;-)

3. What should you keep in mind when installing Pi-Hole?
    1. Nothing else.
    2. Assign a static IP address to the Respberry Pi in the router.
    3. I don't know.

4. What is a DNS provider?
    1. A DNS provider translates IP addresses (192.168.x.x) to domain names (www....).
    2. It provides the latest news.
    3. It provides the current weather data.

5. What are blacklists?
    1. They contain all telephone numbers that play advertising over the Internet and are later blocked by Pi-Hole.
    2. It contains all addresses that play advertisements over the Internet and that are later blocked by Pi-Hole.
    3. I don't know. ;-)

6. How can you access "Pi-Hole" after installation?
    1. With the IP address in the terminal.
    2. With the web address in the terminal.
    3. With the IP address in your browser via "http://IP-Adresse/admin".

Lesson 17: Software Project: Homebridge

1. How can you access "Homebridge" after installation?
   1. Enter "http://IP-Adresse:8080" in the terminal.
   2. Enter "http://IP-Adresse:8080" in your browser
   3. Enter "http://IP-Adresse:8080" in OpenOffice

2. What is the default login?
   1. Username: admin Password: admin
   2. Username: pi Password: get
   3. Username: home Password: bridge

3. Which menu item can you use to add further functions?
   1. The menu item: "Devices".
   2. The menu item: "Config"
   3. The menu item: "Plugins"

Lesson 18: Software Project: Webmin

1. What is the advantage of "Webmin"?
   1. The Raspberry Pi is 50% faster.
   2. The Raspberry Pi can be managed via a graphical user interface.
   3. The Raspberry Pi can be managed over the Internet.

2. What can I do to install software in Webmin?
   1. Via the menu item "System" and then "Software Packages".
   2. Via the menu item Software Updates.

3. Via the "Servers" menu item.

3. How can I create new users on the Raspberry Pi?
   1. Via the "Users" menu item
   2. # Via the menu item "System" and then "Users and Groups".
   3. Via the menu item "Users".

Lesson 19: Software Project: RetroPi (game console) + KODI (media center)

1. What are you turning the Raspberry Pi into with "RetroPi"?
   1. Into a Playstation 4 Clone...
   2. Into an XBox 360 Clone...
   3. In a classic retro game console.

2. Where can you download RetroPi?
   1. www.apple.com
   2. www.retropi.org.uk
   3. www.microsoft.com

3. How do you install RetroPi on the micro SD card?
   1. With the OpenOffice software.
   2. With the Apple Pi Baker software.
   3. With the Software Etcher from Lesson 8.
4. What is recommended for configuring RetroPi?
   1. A connected gamepad.
   2. A connected keyboard.
   3. A connected USB cable.

5. What is "KODI"?
    1. A multimedia center.
    2. A video editing software.
    3. A music player.

6. How can you start KODI from RetroPi?
    1. Select "Games" and then "KODI".
    2. # Select "Ports" and then "KODI".
    3. Select "RetroPi" and then "KODI".

Lesson 20: Hardware based Projects

1. Which sensor kit is recommended to start with?
    1. 37 Sensors and Modules Starter Kit from SunFounder
    2. 12 sensors and modules starter kit from Max
    3. 7 sensors and modules starter kit from Cube

Lesson 21: Hardware Project: Camera Module

1. How many megapixels does the camera module have?
    1. 2 MegaPixel
    2. 5 MegaPixel
    3. 8 MegaPixel

2. At what resolution can the camera module record?
    1. 1080p (FullHD resolution)
    2. 760p (HDReady resolution)

    3. 480p

3. What can the camera module be used as, for example?
    1. Night vision camera
    2. Security camera
    3. Mobile phone camera

4. How do you activate the camera module?
    1. Use the command "sudo raspi-config" and then select "Camera module".
    2. With the command "sudo raspi-config activate camera".
    3. With the command "sudo raspi-config" and then select "Interfacing Options" and "Camera".

5. Which command is used to create a new photo?
    1. raspistill -o image.jpg
    2. raspi-config -o image.jpg
    3. raspi -o image.jpg

6. What command do you use to create a video?
    1. createvid -t 10000 -o video.h264
    2. raspivid -t 10000 -o video.h264
    3. create -t 10000 -o video.h264

Lesson 22: Hardware Project: Humidity Sensor

1. To what must "VCC" be connected?

1. To the power.
2. To the data pin.
3. On Ground.

2. To what must "GND" be connected?
1. To Ground.
2. To the data PIN.
3. To the power.

3. What must "DO" be connected to?
1. To the data PIN.
2. To the power.
3. To the ground.

Lesson 23: Hardware Project: Light Sensor
Learn how to use a light sensor on the Raspberry Pi.

1. What should the yellow cable be connected to on the Raspberry Pi?
1. At PIN 21.
2. At PIN 1.
3. At PIN 2.

2. In which programming language is the script executed?
1. Monty
2. # Python
3. C++

3. What is the name of the program on the Raspberry Pi

with which the script can be opened?
   1. Thonny
   2. Tom
   3. Ben

Lesson 24: Hardware Project: Laser Module
No Quiz-Questions.

Lesson 25: Programming with Scratch

1. What principle does Scratch work with?
   1. Modular principle
   2. Sandbox principle
   3. Universal principle

2. For whom was Scratch originally designed for?
   1. For adults and seniors.
   2. For children and teenagers.
   3. For toddlers.

3. What can you program with Scratch?
   1. Server applications
   2. Databases
   3. Small applications and games.

4. How do you start Scratch?
   1. Via the start menu under "Programming".
   2. From the start menu under "Development".
   3. Via the start menu under the item "Programs".

Lesson 26: Programming with Thonny

1. How do you start the program "Thonny"?
    1. From the start menu under "Games".
    2. From the start menu under "Help".
    3. From the start menu under "Development"

2. Which programming language does Thonny use for programming?
    1. Python1
    2. Python2
    3. Python3

3. Can you run programs in Thonny directly?
    1. Yes.
    2. No.
    3. I don't know.

4. Where can you directly execute commands?
    1. In the area "Bin".
    2. In the "Shell" area.
    3. In the area "Bash".

5. What else can be programmed with Thonny?
    1. Sensors and modules connected to the Raspberry Pi.
    2. Windows Programs
    3. Mac Applications

Quiz-Answers

1. Raspberry Pi Foundation in England (UK)

2. 2012

3. 17 Million pieces

4. It's size in credit card format.

5. To introduce young people and pupils to programming.

6. LibreELEC, HomeBridge, MagicMirror, Pi-Hole, RetroPi

7. Filter out advertising

8. Run a multimedia center, listen to internet radio, watch movies, etc.

9. Home automation such as controlling lamps from a mobile phone.

10. LibreELEC, HomeBridge, MagicMirror, Pi-Hole, RetroPi

11. Filter out advertising

12. Run a multimedia center, listen to internet radio, watch movies, etc.

13. Raspberry Pi 3B+

14. 1GB of RAM

15. Yes.

16. Raspberry Pi Zero

17. Raspberry Pi 3B+

18. microSD card

19. 32GB

20. It should have the speed class 10.

21. 37 Modules and Sensors Starter Kit from Sunfounder

22. With the original Raspberry Pi power supply.

23. Processor, main memory, graphics card

24. From 70 degrees.

25. 1GB of RAM.

26. 400 Mhz

27. It is also a composite video connector.

28. This chip provides Wifi and Bluetooth functionality.

29. On the lower side of the Raspberry Pi 3B+.

30. 3 watts per hour.

31. Libre Office Suite, Chromium web browser, small games etc.

32. Raspbian

33. By clicking on the raspberry at the top left corner.

34. Scratch und Python

35. Linux (Debian)

36. At www.raspberrypi.org/downloads/

37. A graphical installation program for the Raspberry Pi operating system.

38. This version includes a graphical user interface and recommended software.

39. This version does not include a graphical user interface.

40. Ubuntu MATE

41. Install NOOBS.

42. Download the operating system Raspbian.

43. It writes the Raspbian operating system to the microSD card.

44. Unzip the NOOBS .zip file and copy the files to the microSD card.

45. Insert the microSD card into the Raspberry Pi and start the Raspberry Pi.

46. The NOOBS installation interface

appears.

47. With select "Raspbian (recommended)" and click on "Install".

48. The WLAN settings.

49. Username: pi Password: raspberry

50. The suggested software updates. Command: sudo apt-get upgrade & apt-get update

51. SSH

52. Simply create a file named "ssh" on the microSD card on the "boot" partition.

53. In my router, with LANScan (Mac) or Advanced IP Scanner (PC).

54. ssh <IP address> -l pi

55. sudo raspi-config

56. The "Locale" settings to the region EN/USA and then the "Wi-Fi Country" settings to EN/USA.

57. VNC

58. Via the RealVNC Viewer program.

59. Apple Pi Baker

60. Win32 Disk Imager

61. If something goes wrong, I can restore the saved image with all settings immediately.

62. Yes.

63. SD Card Formatter

64. To cleanly erase all data on the SD card.

65. A network-wide ad blocker.

66. Connect Smarthome devices to Apple's HomeKit.

67. A handy user interface for system management.

68. Perform a software update with "sudo apt-get update" and "sudo apt-get

upgrade" on the terminal.

69. Yes.

70. Assign a static IP address to the Raspberry Pi in the router.

71. A DNS provider translates IP addresses (192.168.x.x) to domain names (www....).

72. It contains all addresses that play advertisements over the Internet and that are later blocked by With the IP address in your browser via "http://IP-Adresse/admin".

73. Enter "http://IP-Adresse:8080" in your browser

74. Username: admin Password: admin

75. The menu item: "Plugins"

76. The Raspberry Pi can be managed via a graphical user interface.

77. Via the menu item "System" and then

"Software Packages".

78. Via the menu item "System" and then "Users and Groups".

79. In a classic retro game console.

80. www.retropi.org.uk

81. With the Software Etcher from Lesson 8.

82. A connected gamepad.

83. A multimedia center.

84. Select "Ports" and then "KODI".

85. 37 Sensors and Modules Starter Kit from SunFounder

86. 8 MegaPixel

87. 1080p (FullHD resolution)

88. Security camera

89. With the command "sudo raspi-config"

and then select "Interfacing Options" and "Camera".

90. raspistill -o image.jpg

91. raspivid -t 10000 -o video.h264

92. To the power.

93. To Ground.

94. To the data PIN.

95. At PIN 21.

96. Python

97. Thonny

98. Modular principle

99. For children and teenagers.

100. Small applications and games.

101. Via the start menu under "Programming".

102. From the start menu under

"Development"

103. Python3

104. Yes.

105. In the "Shell" area.

106. Sensors and modules connected to the Raspberry Pi.

28. Access to the Video Lessons

For this book, the 25 video lessons were developed at www.raspi-config.com/amazon

Here you can watch all book chapters again in video format:

Login: www.raspi-config.com/amazon
Password: AMAZON BOOK

Made in the USA
Coppell, TX
29 May 2021